Travels of a Grape

By M.C. Hall

Scott Foresman
is an imprint of

Glenview, Illinois • Boston, Massachusetts • Chandler, Arizona •
Upper Saddle River, New Jersey

Photographs

Every effort has been made to secure permission and provide appropriate credit for photographic material. The publisher deeply regrets any omission and pledges to correct errors called to its attention in subsequent editions.

Unless otherwise acknowledged, all photographs are the property of Pearson Education, Inc.

Photo locators denoted as follows: Top (T), Center (C), Bottom (B), Left (L), Right (R), Background (Bkgd)

1 (T,B) Jupiter Images; **3** (R) ©David Murray/©DK Images, (R) ©Philip Dowell/©DK Images; **4** ©Ingram Publishing/Getty Images; **5** (C) ©DK Images, (R) ©Philip Dowell/©DK Images; **6** ©Philip Dowell/©DK Images; **7** Inga Spence/Visuals Unlimited/Getty Images; **8** ©Tim Graham/Getty Images; **9** ©Ed Young/Corbis; **10** ©Jim Sugar/Corbis; **11** ©Arthur Schatz/Time Life Pictures/Getty Images; **12** ©Ian O'Leary/©DK Images; **13** ©FrÈdÈric Neema/Sygma/Corbis; **14** (B) ©Markos Dolopikos/Alamy, (B) Jupiter Images; **15** (T) ©DK Images, (BR) Jupiter Images, (BL) ©Pete Seaward/Stone/Getty Images; **16** ©Image Source; Global (Bkgd) ©David Murray/©DK Images, (Bkgd) Philip Dowell/©DK Images.

ISBN 13: 978-0-328-47293-2
ISBN 10: 0-328-47293-X

4 5 6 7 8 9 10 V010 13 12

Table of Contents

At the Grocery Store

Our grocery stores are filled with fresh fruits and vegetables. There are crunchy carrots and bright red peppers. There are bunches of bananas and green and purple grapes.

Who grows the fruits and vegetables we buy to eat? How do these foods get to our stores? Let's find out.

The grapes we eat are called *table grapes.* In the United States, almost all table grapes are grown in California. Each American eats about eight pounds of grapes a year! We'll go to California, where most grapes start their trip.

These grapes traveled thousands of miles from where they were grown.

Resources at Work

It takes many resources to grow the foods we eat. Grapes and other food plants need natural resources such as soil and water.

This irrigation system sprays water onto the fields. Water flows through ditches to the plants.

Grapes grow on vines in fields called *vineyards.* The vines need a lot of water. If there isn't enough rain, farmers use irrigation systems to bring water to the plants.

People are another important resource needed to grow grapes. Farmers dig up fields and plant the grapevines. Workers pull weeds that could choke the vines. They trim the vines so they will grow the right way.

Workers set stakes to support young grapevines.

After the fruit starts to grow, workers cut off dead leaves. When the grapes are ripe, it's harvest time. Workers cut bunches of grapes from the vines. They put the grapes into boxes or crates. Then they load the boxes onto wagons or carts.

Workers have to be careful not to bruise the fruit.

Migrant workers are often hired to pick grapes. Migrant workers move from place to place to find work. They come to vineyards when the grapes are ripe.

When these workers finish picking grapes, they'll move on to another place to pick a different crop.

When Cesar Chavez was a child, he and his family were migrant farm workers. They had to move often to find work. Sometimes Cesar had to skip school to work. Migrant workers were paid very little, so the Chavez family was very poor.

When Cesar grew up, he formed a group called the United Farm Workers. He worked for better pay and safer jobs for migrant farm workers.

Cesar Chavez did not want young children to work in the fields.

Grapes on the Move

Now the grapes are ready for their long trip. Workers load them onto special refrigerated trucks or train cars. Some grapes go to other places around the world. Those grapes are shipped on airplanes in refrigerated containers. The cool temperatures keep the grapes fresh.

The grapes in these crates are ready to go all the way across the United States!

The refrigerated grapes leave California and travel to cities all across the United States. Then smaller trucks pick up the grapes. They take them to nearby farm stands and grocery stores.

From Vineyard to Store

Grapes grow in vineyards.

Workers put grapes out to sell.

Workers pick ripe grapes.

Refrigerated trucks take grapes across the country.

Smaller trucks carry grapes to stores.

Fruit on the Table

These grapes aren't done traveling yet, even though they've already come thousands of miles to get to your store. The last step is buying them, bringing them home, and washing them. Now they're truly ready for their final "home"–inside YOU!